SEVEN REASONS TO HIRE AN ATTORNEY

*Protecting Your
Workers' Compensation Benefits*

JAMES W. ARMSTRONG JR.

Lillies of the Field LLC

Seattle Washington

SEVEN REASONS TO HIRE AN ATTORNEY

Protecting Your Workers' Compensation Benefits

Washington State Edition

This booklet is provided through Armstrong Law Offices to help you learn how an attorney can help protect your claim for benefits.

If you have any questions, please call our law offices at (253) 854-7343.

We can help.

Copyright © 2014-16 James W. Armstrong Jr.

Published by Lillies of the Field LLC
All rights reserved.

ISBN: 1495340228
ISBN-13: 978-1495340222

Please note that this book is not meant to replace obtaining a lawyer and does not serve as legal advice.

SEVEN REASONS TO HIRE AN ATTORNEY

Protecting Your Workers' Compensation Benefits

Contents

Acknowledgments vi

Why Choose an Attorney to Represent You and Your Claim? 1

   What You Gain by Reading This Booklet 1

   What You Find in This Booklet 1

   What's Important about Having an Attorney 2

Benefit #1: Claim Management 3

Benefit #2: Representation for Self-Insured Claims 5

Benefit #3: Your Independent Medical Examination 7

Benefit #4: Responding to a Denial of Treatment 9

Benefit #5: Assignment of Vocational Counselor 11

Benefit #6: Managing Closing Orders 13

Benefit #7: Appealing Rejected Claims 15

What Can Your Attorney Do for You and Your Claim? 17

Frequently Asked Questions 19

About the Author 21

Acknowledgments

I would like to thank God for allowing me to practice law for the past 14 years. During this time, I have had the opportunity to continue to assist those in need. Stephen Matlock, a great friend, not only encouraged me to write this book but supported me along the way with his guidance. Lastly I want to thank those who are taking time to read this book. May it give you information to assist you in your case.

Why Choose an Attorney to Represent You and Your Claim?

The first thing to ask yourself is this: do you need an attorney to represent your claim? To answer that question you must know several things about you and your claim.

When you understand the skill, expertise, and value an attorney brings to managing your claim, you can be prepared to engage your attorney.

What You Gain by Reading This Booklet

By reading this material, you will understand the following benefits:

1. What you gain from hiring an attorney to represent your interests
2. What to expect when your attorney becomes your advocate before the Department of Labor and Industries
3. What you will be asked to do in order to obtain your benefits with as few delays as possible

What You Find in This Booklet

Topics covered in this booklet include the following:

- Claim Management
- Self-Insured Claims
- Your Independent Medical Examination
- Denial of Treatment

- Assignment of Vocational Counselor
- Closing Orders
- Rejected Claims

What's Important about Having an Attorney

Your Workers' Compensation claim is important to you for these three reasons:

1. Your claim is your only opportunity to make a statement regarding your injuries and associated benefits.
2. Receiving timely benefits without delay reduces the chances of lasting effects of your injuries.
3. Continuing to receive compensation while you are unable to work relieves the stress of being out of work while suffering from work related injuries.

Benefit #1: Claim Management

You gain a number of advantages when you hire an attorney to **manage your claim**, the most significant of which is that you can avoid the remaining six reasons to need an attorney!

When you have the assistance and resources of an experienced attorney and his staff, your claim is actively managed by people who know what to anticipate and how to prepare for challenges. This relieves you of the stress of not only simply waiting for something to happen but not being prepared to move quickly when the process demands it.

An attorney familiar with similar claims can reasonably predict the likely next steps that must be taken on your claim. Monthly reviews and status updates will keep your attorney current with your claim as well as the actions needed to keep your claim moving along in the process.

Of course, having an attorney representing you will not prevent every adverse decision, but he/she will definitely prepare you to address any challenges that may arise during the life of your claim.

In the end, though an attorney may take a fee, it is worth the representation, especially if your benefits are threatened. An attorney does not take a fee from benefits that are denied or delayed.

JAMES W. ARMSTRONG JR.

Benefit #2: Representation for Self-Insured Claims

A **Self-Insured Claim** is a claim that arises when the employer carries its own insurance and hires a third party to manage the claim. If you have a self-insured claim and you think it's open-and-shut, think again. However, if by chance everything goes well for you, you receive the recommended treatment, vocational retraining, etc., you may not need the services of an attorney and your case will settle.

Most cases are not open-and-shut. This applies to the cases you might think are the simplest and easiest to understand. Most benefits which arise through self-insured claims are challenged by the self-insured employer.

You should know that your employer will have a professional there to represent them on your case. Ask yourself, who will be there representing you?

The third-party administrator is not there to protect you or to understand your issues. Sometimes it seems that once you are injured, shortly thereafter the third-party administrator begins the process to shut down your claim.

One of the first things your employer will utilize is the Independent Medical Examination (IME). Quite often, they will schedule an IME more frequently than what's typical for a State Fund claim (claims managed by the Department). Or, they will schedule the IME a short time after you have begun to receive treatment, and before you could be expected to have received any benefits from those treatments. Such an IME would not show your true condition, and might lead to a reduction or denial of benefits.

Benefit #3: Your Independent Medical Examination

An **Independent Medical Examination** (IME) is an examination scheduled by the Department as well as by self-insured employers in an attempt to secure medical opinions which may ultimately assist in the shutting down your claim. Many times the doctors who perform these IMEs are the same doctors who have performed these examinations for the Department and Self-Insured Employers for many years. As such, keep in mind the source of the referral.

After the IME takes place, your doctor is sent a copy for his agreement. If your doctor does not agree, you will be sent out to yet another IME to break the "tie" between your doctor and the IME doctor. Once the results from the second examination come back and they are adverse to you, the process to shut down your claim will continue until your claim is closed now that there are two separate IME doctors giving adverse opinions opposite your treating doctor.

How we can help? If you are sent to an IME, yes, that report will be sent to your doctor. If your doctor does not agree with the IME, we will schedule another examination, before the Department or self-insured employer does, so you can obtain an objective opinion from someone who is not potentially compromised by the Department or the third-party administrator who have utilized their services many times in the past.

If that objective opinion comes back in your favor, we will submit that along with your own doctor's agreement to the Department. This will aid in getting your claim back on track so you continue to receive time-loss compensation, vocational services, necessary medical treatment, and any other benefits you are entitled to receive.

Benefit #4: Responding to a Denial of Treatment

Denial of Treatment can occur as the result of three events:
1. After a recent IME which states that your treatment has concluded and finds you fixed and stable.
2. After the recent scheduling of an IME matched with the unwillingness of either the Department or the self-insured employer to continue to provide treatment until such an examination takes place.
3. After an analysis of your medical file which shows no recent objective evidence to justify the continued need for further necessary and proper treatment.

To help you avoid a Denial of Treatment, your attorney will make sure he/she stays up-to-date with your current medical information. He/She will also argue that the current medical opinion in your file states you are in need of medical treatment. As such, until an IME takes place indicating otherwise, the opinion that treatment is necessary remains in effect. If need be, your attorney will work with your claim manager to ensure treatment continues in exchange for your attendance at an upcoming IME.

JAMES W. ARMSTRONG JR.

Benefit #5: Assignment of Vocational Counselor

Once you are determined to be fixed and stable (i.e., treatment is no longer necessary) and you have received restrictions from your doctor, a **Vocational Counselor** will be assigned to your case as a determination regarding your return to work will need to be made.

If retraining is necessary to return you to the workforce, your attorney will help you choose a retraining goal that fits your skills and interests.

Without an attorney to stand up for you and to focus attention on you, the injured party, an often-overworked or unmotivated Vocational Counselor, may seek to place you in positions such as general clerk, electronic assembler, and so on—positions usually not attractive to most retraining candidates.

Your attorney should work ensure you receive your two-year retraining plan instead of a two-month on-the-job training plan that will prove to place you at a disadvantage when you seek a job upon the completion of your program.

JAMES W. ARMSTRONG JR.

Benefit #6: Managing Closing Orders

Once your claim closes, you will receive a **Closing Order** with appeal rights. If you disagree with the closing order, you have 60 days to protest or appeal the decision. It cannot be emphasized enough—**seeking counsel is a must at this point**. Submitting a protest to the claim closure without legal advice may lead to the scheduling of yet another IME. Without legal advice you will attend this IME and have yet another opinion against you, making it even more difficult to have the closing order reversed on appeal.

However, if you receive a closing order and contact an attorney, he/she can assist in making the correct decision regarding the manner in which to proceed. There may be medical information that has been overlooked in the file making a protest of the closure appropriate. In most cases, an appeal will be the more appropriate route to take so as not to be exposed to another IME.

Remember, the Department or your self-insured employer will have a trained, experienced attorney to represent their interests once an appeal is filed. For your own protection, **hiring an attorney will increase your chances for success in securing further benefits**.

JAMES W. ARMSTRONG JR.

Benefit #7: Appealing Rejected Claims

Claims filed with the Department may be denied for a number of reasons:

- Perhaps the required medical documentation which relates your injury to your job is missing or is not complete. In this case, your attorney can properly analyze your case, determine what if anything is missing or incomplete and take the appropriate action.
- Perhaps the Department has sent you to an IME, the results of which led to a rejection of your claim. (This second examination may have been requested, even though your application was submitted by a separate physician who examined you for your condition.)

If your claim is rejected, you may protest. After the protest is filed however, the Department will more than likely schedule another IME even if one was already performed.

If your claim has already been rejected, you should not attend a subsequent examination. Attending an IME at the request of the Department when they have already rejected the claim gives them yet another opportunity to obtain information to support their previous rejection. If you attend the IME, that medical opinion, coupled with the first IME, will be difficult to overcome on appeal.

A better approach is to make a direct appeal to the **Board of Industrial Insurance Appeals**. Your direct appeal will get the claim out of the hands of the Department or Third-Party Administrator and will prevent them from sending you to yet another examination to obtain additional information to strengthen their decision to reject your claim.

What Can Your Attorney Do for You and Your Claim?

An attorney who specializes in claim management can help you focus on what is important to you—your claim—but will do the hard work of moving your claim through the process more quickly and efficiently.

Your attorney also will protect your interests so you get the maximum benefits guaranteed under law.

We can help! All the steps listed here will take place on your claim whether or not you are prepared for them.

Will you have an attorney to protect your interests, or will you place yourself behind the 8-ball until your claim is too far gone to salvage?

Get an attorney. Hire us. We can help.

We *will* help.

Contact us at
www.Armstrong-LawOffice.com
or by telephone at (253) 854-7343

JAMES W. ARMSTRONG JR.

Frequently Asked Questions

I've been hurt at work. What do I do?

If you are hurt at work, contact your immediate supervisor, go see "your own" doctor (not a doctor your employer directs you to see) and complete an application for benefits

I've been off work and haven't received an L&I payment. Are there steps I need to take?
- Complete worker verification form and submit to L&I;
- Make a doctor's appointment and make sure your doctor has taken you off work;
- Contact your Claim Manager with dates of doctor appointment so she/he can keep an eye out for that chart note.

My employer has offered me light duty. Am I required to accept the job?

While there is no requirement to accept a light-duty job, be aware that if you do not accept light duty, you will not be eligible for time loss compensation unless at some point you are totally taken off work as opposed to being released to light duty.

Is my employer required to accommodate my restrictions with a light duty job?

Your employer is not required to offer you light duty. If your employer does not have a light duty to offer, you will be eligible for time loss compensation

My claim closed and I did not appeal the claim closure. Can I reopen my claim?

You can apply to reopen your claim up to 7 years from the date of the first claim closure. Keep in mind that your condition has to have objectively worsened for the claim to be reopened.

I was injured on the job and taken off work by my doctor but terminated by my employer. Am I eligible for time loss compensation?

You are eligible for time loss compensation even if you are terminated from your job if the termination was without cause and you have medical certification to be off work.

If I receive a settlement, will it be in one lump sum?

If you receive a permanent partial disability award (PPD), you will receive a down payment (the amount to be determined based on date of injury). You will receive monthly payments with interest until the entire PPD is paid in full. After 70 days has passed and the closing order has become final and binding, you can request that the entire PPD balance be paid. It will be paid minus interest.

About the Author

JAMES W. ARMSTRONG JR. has been an attorney for fourteen years. His firm, Armstrong Law Offices, focuses on workers' compensation and Social Security disability.

Armstrong served for four years in the United States Marine Corps, received his Bachelor's Degree from Western Washington University, and earned his law degree from Seattle University School of Law.

You can reach him at www.Armstrong-LawOffice.com or by phone at (253) 854-7343

JAMES W. ARMSTRONG JR.

www.ingramcontent.com/pod-product-compliance
Lightning Source LLC
Chambersburg PA
CBHW070733180526
45167CB00004B/1733